Poppy's Poems

VOLUME II: WHIMSICAL WISDOM

ROBERT G. LAPOINTE

POPPY'S POEMS

VOLUME II: WHIMSICAL WISDOM

ISBN: 978-1-0688528-3-1 (Paperback)
ISBN: 978-1-0688528-5-5 (Hardcover)
ISBN: 978-1-0688528-4-8 (Ebook)

Cover Design and Illustrations by: Rein G.

Layout Design by: Rein G.
@reindrawthings (www.fiverr.com)

For Our Peanut,
who we love and miss every day.

TABLE OF CONTENTS

~Wins~

GIVE AND TAKE

In life stay focused.
Your goals do review.
Enjoy each moment.
Screen everything new.

Always be humble.
Accept with a smile
Compliments coming
Reflecting your style.

Give help when you can.
Welcome your dreams.
Share your life's interests
On bright rainbow beams.

Always say never.
Just never say no.
Never say always.
Enjoy your life's flow.

Who will be watching
When our lives we live ?
We should remember –
"Take Less Than We Give !"

YOUR VOICE

Thanks for the chat.
We loved your voice.
Talking to us,
Was a nice choice.

All four chairs turned.
Our anxious smile
Said "Join my team;
Come stay awhile."

Please speak to us
Of things you do,
At school and home,
Both old and new.

Are your days full ?
Projects galore ?
Gray Matter used,
So much, much more ?

Be Proud ! Move On !
Share everything !
Your life's a song,
So let it sing.

BONJOUR

Every day's a new day
Because I make it so.
If you travel with me
I'll show how it will go.

I just take a language
And speak it for two days.
Spanish is my first choice,
For I know all their ways.

French would be my second choice.
Two days again I'd speak.
Mastering this language
Would be the goal I seek.

Challenging my English,
With Agatha's mystery scenes
Helps me be creative
As I learn what my life means.

Two weeks for my English
With visuals to enjoy,
Will be entertaining
When, my skills, I employ.

Now I have a system
To repeat through the year.
My imagination
Is what I hold so dear.

New skills I will master.
Excitement there will be.
Only if my speaking
Includes a memory.

A JOY TO SEE

What's this I hear ?
To be a star,
You're learning to
Play the guitar.

Let fingers fly,
Just like your Dad.
Practice pays off.
You will be glad.

Just watch Dad play
And listen well.
Techniques he'll show.
Secrets he'll tell.

Time, it will take,
As all things do,
To master what,
To you is new.

"I CAN'T", is not
A phrase you'll hear.
Practice ! Enjoy !
Wear a smile, Dear !

I know, in time
All things will be
The way you want,
A joy to see.

WE MAKE OUR OWN FUTURE

We make our own Future.
This we should believe.
Just search your own memory
And knowledge retrieve.

To look at what happened
And what came before
Will help in your vision
Just open the door.

For now you can study.
The patterns you make
Do improve what you see.
Your future's at stake.

Conclusions may vary.
There's no guarantee
That with this new knowledge
Your future you'll see.

Sharing with a close friend
With what's on your mind
May help with the challenge.
Solutions you'll find.

Of course the opinion
That's behind your door
May be rather shallow –
Worth not to explore.

We make our own Future
This we do agree
The fun we should cherish
Whatever will be.

Decisions we do make.
Just sit back and rest.
Observe what's in your view
For life is a test.

ON THE ROAD AGAIN

Toronto Read,
A Photo Shoot,
Costumes to pick,
All nice and cute.

Acting your lines
While on the set,
Is the most fun
That you'll have yet.

So much you'll learn.
Just look around,
For there's great knowledge
To be found.

Take a deep breath
And listen well.
Where this will lead
Is hard to tell.

Do celebrate
Your newfound friends.
Just be yourself
Til story ends.

There's more to come.
Embrace what's new.
And always take
Our love with you !

A DAY OF DAYS

A day of days –
What I did see
Was gratitude
Direct to me –

For my hard work –
For efforts grand –
So graciously
Was a big hand.

So proud I am
Yet humble too –
Knowing my work
Is in review.

Some days I know
For me will shine –
Some dreams come true –
All will be mine.

Some days I know
Will challenge more
My time I've spent
But less adore.

Reasons I know
Aren't always clear
For in life "all"
We don't revere.

My tears of joy
I do caress.
Those other tears
Do cause some stress.

But lessons learned
Both old and new
Provide for me
A pleasant view.

Each day I ride
My ups and downs
With smiles I see –
At times some frowns.

My Lifelong Rule –
"Enjoy Each Day" –
My love Galore
I send your way.

ANOTHER YEAR

Another year
For all to see –
Such precious time
You share with me.

Each minute counts
That fills the day.
Please love all love
That comes your way.

New ventures stay.
Old ventures go.
Sometimes they mix
With what we know.

A gentle smile
You share with all.
New memories
We all recall.

Priorities !
We view your style.
Every which way,
Now and awhile.

We trust this gift
Will get you through
Some rainy days.
Enjoy each view.

ON YOUR MARK

Your sneakers tight
With double knots –
Just make sure to
Connect the dots.

A weather cast –
What should you wear
On your journey
From here to there ?

A rested mind
A dream come true –
It's nice to try
Something that's new.

Early to bed –
Dream brand new dreams –
Relax – Enjoy
All that it seems.

Special effects
A Rainbow Bright
Your 10K Race
Brings much delight.

You could jog home
After the race,
But "NO" I think
Is on your face.

So just cool down
With H_2O –
A job well done –
Where next to go ?

THE BEST OF DAYS

Another Year
Another Day
Nice memories
Did come your way.

A visit too
Some friends of old –
New ventures shared –
Old ventures told.

The best of days
You did relate.
We're sure you did
Participate.

New challenges –
New Dreams and More
You will create –
You will adore !

Whatever comes
Know this is true –
Our love each day
Will shadow you.

PHASE TWO

New ventures await you.
The future does hold
A world full of wonder
Each day you unfold.

This journey inspires
Your creative ways.
Be assured your parents
Will fill up some days.

New challenges do bring
Some gifts into view.
These pleasures do surely
Appear to be new.

Deserving ? Don't question !
For we all agree
That your happiness does
Reflect a journey.

That in life, your sharing
Does honor us all.
Fond memories we cherish
Our love please recall.

CAN WE COME TOO ?

Shiver ! Shiver !
Morning sun.
You'll be glad
When this is done.

Acting is grand –
So much to see.
These thoughts are warm.
Soon warm I'll be !

The day slides by,
Adventures new –
Each minute, learn –
Embrace the view.

You choose what lens ?
What's colored bright ?
What carries you
Into the night ?

A day of rest
Awaits your bones.
Light exercise,
Your body tones.

Another script –
A part to take.
An actor's dream –
Choices to make.

Like life itself,
You're on a stage.
Take us along.
Please turn the page.

GOLLY GEES

Create your own person –
Not too big or small.
Provide all life's answers
You choose to recall.

Solutions for many –
Solutions for few –
Fear less on your journey.
Try something that's new.

Create your own person.
Share what your mind sees.
Solve many life issues.
Count your "Golly Gees !"

Present your solutions
Just "slow" as you go
Share your words of wisdom
Based on what you know.

Enjoy your creation.
Some humor, please bring –
Be proud of your efforts
In most everything.

GRADUATION

We're proud of all the work you've done.
We're glad that you had so much fun.
Next year a new grade you will see.
Grade one will make you most happy.

There'll be fun things for you to do.
Reading, writing, and math problems too.
You'll see old friends. They'll make you smile.
You'll dress for school in your own style.

This summer read most every day.
Take time to go outside to play.
Help mommy keep the house real neat,
So things don't bump into your feet.

Visit Nana and Poppy too.
Go on long walks. Enjoy the view.
A hug and kiss we send your way.
Enjoy your graduation day.

BELIEVE

Whatever I'm doing
Wherever I go
I take with me memories
Of all that I know.

I add to the tower
Of thoughts that I keep.
Some do bring me laughter.
Some do make me weep.

A journey well taken
I look forward to.
Some travels repeated
Or a journey new.

With customs and cuisine
Quite new to my bite
I cautiously do choose
For the best delight.

Each venture does carry
It's own special dreams.
Reliving vacations
Brings more joy it seems.

When sharing with family
Each moment in time
The love that surrounds us
Will make church bells chime.

Each distance we travel
Each surface we walk
Each air that we breathe in
Gives reason to talk.

Go shopping together
At a city mall
Create on these travels
Tall tales to recall.

A good day for ice cream –
We'll hop in the car.
Short journeys like this do
Create a new star.

For under the moonlight
Or bright shining sky
Each Minute – Each Moment
On thoughts we rely.

Great Food and Great Workouts
Give us "Daily Bread"
Which surely reminds us –
Our Grey Matter is Fed.

In life there's a journey.
Much good we receive.
Remember to pay back –
This we should believe !

~Woes~

LIFE

I've found that life
Has challenges
Beyond what I
Can see.

I've found that life
Has mysteries
To solve, and some
By me !

I've found that life
Has many friends
To help along
The way.

I've found that life
Has Mother's love
That I caress
Each day.

I've found that life
Has offerings
With choices to
Be made.

I've found that life
Has penalties
If the cookie jar
I raid !

I've found that life
Has moments when
Some pain is what
I feel.

I've found that life
Creates a time
When comfort is
So Real !

I've found that life
Presents itself
With certain gifts
So dear !

I've found that life
Has happiness
Now and throughout
The Year !

ENJOY THE VIEW

Enjoy what comes
Your way each day.
New messages,
Time will relay.

Some challenges
You will enjoy.
There will be some
That do annoy.

Regardless of
What's in your view,
Always, our love
Will be there too.

DEEP THOUGHTS

I just have too many things.
I'm running out of space.
If I make just one more buy,
For me they'll be no place.

What I have and what I want
And what I really need,
All have different characters.
Their values change indeed.

I will have to sit way back
Just to evaluate
What my wardrobe does involve.
I best not hesitate !

Lots of glitter ! Lots of lace !
Some gorgeous clothes I see.
It is, oh so evident
That people do love me.

When I look around my world
It brings to me a smile.
How fortunate it is to know
I live in such grand style.

Rather than so many "things"
To keep me company,
Maybe I could be content
With friends and family.

But, if, in fact, I cannot choose
Which clothes I plan to keep,
I will ask my Mom and Dad,
To build my closet "deep".

GERTRUDE THE RAINDROP REVISITED

So many raindrops –
Each has their own name
But in a shower
They all look the same.

Pounding the rooftop –
Just crushing the land
Flooding of my world
That I find most grand.

Birds will seek shelter –
Protecting their young
Knowing their nesting
Is securely hung.

All of Earth's creatures
Will do what they do
To journey safely
Throughout Nature's Zoo.

So many dark skies
With clouds filled with rain
Is stressful to all –
No rest does remain.

Those who live under
An umbrella world
Softly do cuddle
Safely they're curled.

Protection we're searching
When lightning appears
With cymbal warnings
It's thunder one hears.

The roots of our world
Do welcome the gift
That raindrops do give –
Providing life's lift.

Too much of Nature –
Sometimes we agree –
Does bring us more harm
Than we'd like to see.

GERTRUDE, my raindrop,
Lives with one great fear –
"To land in a puddle
Where dogs wander near !"

Please avoid life's puddles
That do come your way.
May you journey safely
Each and every day !

GEORGIA ON YOUR MIND

A great challenge,
A new date,
A southern voice,
You must relate.

For all to see,
You bring great joy.
Such dedication
You employ.

Each time you learn
Another skill,
You do embrace
Another thrill.

So fill your days
With everything
That soothes your soul
And makes you sing.

PLEASE LOOK AROUND

Please look around.
What do you see ?
I hope there is
A pose of me.

Please look around.
Is Nana near ?
To you she is
Your special dear.

Please look around.
Find Uncle Mike.
A hug from you,
He'd really like.

Please look around.
Where's Mom and Dad ?
They fill your view.
You're SO ! SO ! Glad !

Please look around.
Your friends do smile.
Enjoy their warmth,
Now and awhile.

Please look around.
"Your" world you've found.
It's filled with clouds,
Earth, Air, and Sound.

Enjoy what is.
Create your own.
Adventure forth,
In "Your" time zone.

One of a kind,
You are my dear.
Try anything.
Have little fear.

Be "smart" for sure,
Select with care,
Just safe journeys.
Avoid a "DARE".

Please be proud
In what you do.
Our love, for sure,
Will follow you.

YOU AND I

Journeys Taken –
Smiles to share
New adventures
Do I dare ?

Of Challenges,
Both old and new
I'm anxious to –
Take in the view.

I see all things
But yet not all.
I forget what
I can't recall.

Much more to do –
Much more to see.
For I'm not sure
What I will be.

Many careers –
That is for sure.
So much to learn –
I will endure.

While making dreams
Both day and night,
My life will be
Of much delight.

New memories,
More than a few.
A quick glance, I
Will share with you.

Seek your own dreams
Do show a smile.
To all the world
Now and awhile.

Your eyes do tell
What you hold dear.
Please share these views
Each Day ! Each Year !

Anxious we are,
Both you and I.
Let's travel well
Beyond the SKY !

THE SHADOW

One day from the shadows
A voice filled the air.
The words were a whisper –
A Warning – BEWARE !

Some goose bumps did travel
Up and Down my back.
A hero I am not.
It's courage I lack !

A whisper from my voice
Was halted a bit
"For more understanding
I thought I could get."

The Shadow did answer
Much louder this time.
The message was clearer.
"BEWARE !" it did chime.

I could wait no longer.
My courage did grow
From wanting to be safe.
I just had to know !

So, into the Shadow
My body did seek
A voice with a mystery –
The one who did speak !

The deeper I entered
The wider my eyes
Did search for an answer –
And to my surprise

The "Shadow's" behind me –
"BEWARE" is quite clear.
It's "CAUTION" I do take
While I disappear.

Deeper on my journey
Some light leads the way.
A list of the "BEWARES"
Are now on display.

As I read the warnings
I become quite aware
That the Shadow's voice is
A "Friendly Beware."

A message of Caution –
"My health don't ignore
For I have so many
Days left to explore."

The voice in the Shadow
Still scares me a bit –
But "Wisdom" it's sharing
And "Knowledge" I get !

I'll tend to each challenge
That helps make me grow.
This may take a lifetime
So says "The Shadow" !

LOOK UP – LOOK DOWN – LOOK ALL AROUND

Have you ever wondered
What it would be like
To slip on your new boots
And go for a long hike ?

Would it be for hours ?
Would it be for days ?
What would you discover
Roaming Nature's Maze ?

Would you bring a sketch pad ?
A camera would be great.
The more in your backpack
Would surely slow your gait.

Make sure you have water
And a friend or two.
A cell phone fully charged
I'm sure would help you.

Safely walk the main trails.
Your flowers and sunbeams
Will come into focus
To save for future dreams !

Carefully return home.
Share your joy with us.
Check that you have no ticks,
Or we will make a fuss.

PLEASE HOLD MY HAND

So many days
And weeks there are.
So many years
That take us far.

So many dreams
Do fill our view.
So many old –
With memories new.

So many smiles
Do come our way.
So many laughs
Are on display.

So many friends
Do bring us joy.
So many words
Sometimes annoy.

So many gifts
Show people care.
So many hands
We are aware.

So many tears
Sometimes are shed.
So many hearts
Sadness was fed.

So many chores
We have to do.
So many lives
Some Old – Some New.

So many ways
We show what's right.
So many souls
We bring delight.

So many times
Life asks us why.
So many pleas
We do deny.

So many hugs
We should caress.
So many loves
Solve all our stress.

So many walks –
Grateful we stand.
So many steps –
Please Hold My Hand !

OLD TIMES AND NEW

A window cleaned
New World to See
New Songs – New Sights
Eternally !

New Days – New Dawns –
New shelves to Dust –
Soft Breeze to Soothe –
Soft Winds to Gust.

Izzy – New Paws –
Please step just right
"Wet Paint" – Please Read –
Avoid a plight.

Old boxes now
Just hold dead air,
Old House – New House
Both cleaned with care.

"Downsize" a thought
What should be gone ?
Keep only what
You are quite fond.

All schedules NEW –
From here to there.
New times are set
New clothes to wear.

Please watch your step
Both up and down
For slippery socks
Will bring a frown.

New Neighborhood
Once Roger's home –
So many smiles
He's left to roam.

A lovely life
With so much joy –
A diet filled
With Beans and Soy.

On daily drives
New Kids you'll see.
Please be aware
Of their safety.

New goals to set –
Old goals make new.
Embrace the love
That shadows you.

MAYBE I CAN

I caution those
Who do say "no"
To challenges
From their life's flow.

Say "no" to life
And all new things,
Will leave a world
That's void of wings.

Helping others
Will quickly cease.
Your new ideas
Just won't release.

The world just stops.
Nothing is heard.
(A wingless world
Without a bird.)

You'll learn no more.
The mind grows stale.
You question it
To no avail.

Why choose this route ?
Just don't say "no".
"Maybe" is best.
It gives a glow.

To say "Maybe"
Right to your life
Will show the way
To avoid strife.

Problems, many,
And ways to solve,
Brings you a smile
That won't dissolve.

To try something,
Apply your skill.
A joy it brings,
A special thrill.

The world needs you
Most every day.
Your clever mind
Will show the way.

Improve something
That helps "Humankind".
A special cure
You'll surely find.

We're proud, Dear Child
Of what you do.
"Maybe I Can"
Does best suit you.

OUR PEANUT

A broken heart
Has greeted me.
In my world I
No longer see.

Our Peanut left
Her memories
Of daily love –
A look to please !

So many years
Have passed us by.
We ask ourselves –
A saddened why ?

Age did appear
To carry through –
Unwanted grief
Came into view.

We're left with such
Confusing minds.
What do I do
In these sad times ?

No correct way –
No correct wrong
There is to speak
Of those we long.

Our tears say all –
They speak much more
Of Our Peanut
Whom we adore.

Caress we will
The love we share.
Our Peanut, truly
We do care.

The thoughts so deep –
We cherish all
Caressing what
We do recall.

How fortunate
That life did bring
Our Peanut's Love –
Her Everything !

I LOST MY FRIEND

I lost my friend the other day;
I don't know really why.
Some people say my friend is gone
High up into the sky.

I lost my friend the other day
And everywhere I look,
I find a place where we once went
To play or read a book.

I lost my friend the other day;
I'm feeling really sad.
My mind's mixed up, and you know what ?
I'm also very mad.

I lost my friend the other day
And don't know what to do.
I keep looking for my friend;
I'm looking for a clue.

I lost my friend the other day
And I'm beginning to despair.
I'll search around a little more
Because I really care.

There's my friend I could not find,
My friend I could not see.
I found the secret hiding place,
For, my friend's inside of me.

Now I'm feeling happier
Knowing what is true.
My friend is staying in my thoughts;
I now know what to do.

For, every time I'm feeling sad
My nice memories I will ask;
To open up and speak to me
And forever they will last.

CHOICES

The challenges
With each sunrise
Present themselves.
I must stay wise –

For every day
That I do view
I must rely
On thinking through

What may appear
To challenge me.
My life reflects
Reality.

Each moment that
Does pass me by
Provides a chance
For asking "WHY ?"

Answers do come.
Some may be wrong.
I prefer right
To playing "PONG !"

The North Pole has
No morning sun
So challenges
There should be none.

Except of course
It is a trade.
My energy
Would surely fade.

To make a choice
Will come and go.
Life does reflect
On what I know.

The secret is
To listen well.
Much learning will
Much knowledge tell.

Smart choices made
I do recall
Will be the best
For one and all.

~Wonders~

ASK YOURSELF

Ask yourself most every day
When you view what comes your way
If the smile that you now see
Will be for eternity.

Simple gifts we do receive
That, in life, helps us believe.
Morning skies and sunsets do
Soothe our souls upon review.

Our friendships we do caress
When, in need, we deal with stress.
Life's Gifts – Some – we're unaware –
Yet these moments aren't so rare.

Think about a mystery gift
So kind that your heart did lift.
Think about a calming day
When warm kindness came your way.

Do not doubt what life will be.
Cultivate what you do see.
Make each day yours evermore –
Precious times you do adore.

Be aware of what you give
To assure the life you live
Will bring honor to your name –
So "all smiles" will be the same.

A PLEASANT VIEW

I've made new friends –
Some young – Some old.
Some in between,
Or so I'm told.

So much to learn
So much to share
Just listening
Makes me aware.

Of all that's new –
For in my day –
I cherish life
That comes my way.

Caress I do
The dreams I see,
For in my world
They're part of me.

An avenue –
A busy street –
A crossroad where
My thoughts do meet.

What I might do
What I have done
I hope does fill
My life with fun.

Creative dreams
I do like best.
A time well spent
When I'm at rest.

When I'm awake
My dreams are real
Providing me
With zesty zeal.

I learn to share –
I share to learn
For in my life
There's much I yearn.

I thank you all
For what you do
To give our world
A pleasant view !

THE RIGHT MOVE

With goals well set
With time well spent
You moved away
From Household Rent.

A cardboard box
You did employ.
A Family Plan
You filled with joy.

New goals you'll set.
New smiles you'll share.
Know in your heart
That we'll be there.

A hug – A kiss
Our love we send
To guide you though
Your new year's end.

ALWAYS BE TRUE

I love to love
All that is new.
My memories
I do review.

Some good – Some not.
One thing's for sure,
In life there is
Much to endure.

In every day
There's more to greet.
The joys we wish,
Will all repeat.

Our strength we know
Does serve us well.
With secrets shared,
What will they tell ?

To friends your words –
Always be true.
At home also –
What bothers you.

Most problems solved
With helping hands
Depends on where
Their journey lands.

Advice is free.
Look for a smile.
This should last you
For quite awhile.

Nothing's so bad
That we should fear.
Solutions are
So very near.

Enjoy the view
That comes your way.
Caress this love
Most every day.

Your world's our world.
We both do share
Much happiness
Because we care !

YOUR NEW WORLD

Adventures fill
Your every day
Traveling down
Hollywood way.

New House ! New Yard !
Just so much space
Presents itself
In this here place.

Each morning has
Its own routine.
On "smoothies" mostly
You do lean.

With "Home School" work
And "lines" to learn,
Throughout the day
Your mind will yearn.

For new knowledge,
So you can grow
From your cute nose
Down to your toe.

With "Retro" clothes
You will adore
Your journeys as
You do explore.

Enjoy each day.
Enjoy each week.
We're sure your brain
Won't spring a leak.

But if it does
Please worry not.
Borrow from me.
I've got a lot !

A LOVELY DAY

Two lovely girls
Sharing the day
Learning new things
Every which way.

Two lovely girls
Enjoying the sun
Shopping for food
With sales, two for one.

Two lovely girls
Buying a book
Knowledge to find
The World, take a look.

Two lovely girls
Play laser tag
On the winning team
With the right zig and zag.

Two lovely girls
Tomorrow will be
Styling a studio
For all to see.

Two lovely girls
Stroll hand in hand
Sharing their dreams
As they walk the land.

TRUST

So much to be thankful for
Much in life I do adore
Many smiles will come for sure
Based on what has come before.

Trust, I found helped every day
Making sure that on my way
Journey's end, rewards would pay.
Many "thank you's" I would say.

My turn always will appear
For in life it is quite clear
That the view in my own mirror
Reflects a productive year.

Happiness is what I see
Standing there just before me.
With eyes filled with tears of glee
Is my wish of what will be.

Challenges – There are a few –
Some old and some that are new
Lessons learned – Some to review
Teaching me what I should do.

In life there is much to share –
Much to love and much to care.
A promise we do declare
That one's trust we are aware.

PLEASANT DREAMS

How fortunate for you to see
The joys in life that came to me.
For in grade school and well beyond
On many things I grew quite fond.

Each day had ups – Each day had downs,
Each day was filled with happy sounds.
My world did seem to be a dream –
A journey on a rainbow beam.

Travel Alone or with a Friend –
Each Way Enjoyed – Each Its Own End.
Mistakes were made – Lessons were learned
My character, through life, was earned.

To share one's heart, I understand
That life involves a helping hand.
A Tear – A Hug – A Smile or Two
Creates, for me, a pleasant view.

So many friends have come my way –
Some Close – Some Not – Some Here To Stay.
What I have found throughout the years,
Is all have brought their share of tears.

To dwell upon my cloudy days
Exhausts me in so many ways.
To dwell upon a sun so bright
Relaxes me both day and night.

The choice I make that brings a smile
I do caress now and awhile,
For pleasant dreams, both old and new,
I do deserve and So Do You !

LISTEN MORE SAYS POPPY

Above the clouds,
I know not where,
What would I see
If I were there ?

Would I look back
To view what was ?
The reason why –
Why, just because.

Some things matter
Much more than not.
Better answers
Are sometimes sought.

Perfection is
The Avenue
Well traveled by
Only a few.

Complacency
No "job well done" –
It interferes
With all the fun.

Where is the pride ?
Where is the joy ?
It seems most things
Tend to annoy.

No chance I'll see
If I look back –
A dream of dreams –
For facts I lack.

Eliminate
The I in me.
A misspelled world
I always see.

Just listen more.
The world around
Provides for all
A peaceful sound.

HAPPY CHAPS

Maple Syrup
Melting Snow
Muddy Season
Tulips Grow.

Insects Travel
All Around.
Oddest places
They are found.

Sunscreen Season –
Very Short.
St. Lawrence River
Cold to Court.

White Sand Beaches
Warm My Feet.
Winter's Recessed –
Greet the Heat !

Camping Outdoors –
Breathe Fresh Air –
Striped Guest, You should
Best Beware !

Fall Forever –
Floating Leaves –
Painted Landscape
Busy Bees.

Rake the Front Lawn –
Make a Pile.
Dive into Fun
For a While.

Winter Jackets
Favorite Gloves.
Floating Snowflakes
Filled with Loves.

Snowmen Smiling –
Ski Downhill –
Moonlit Skating –
Winter's Thrill !

Go Full Circle –
Chocolate Chips.
Maple Syrup –
Pancake Bits.

Start All Over –
Fill the Gaps
Twelve Month Voyage –
"HAPPY – CHAPS !"

ENJOY THE MOMENT

Nana says that you are
As busy as a bee,
Doing lots of school stuff.
Your days look full, to me.

Hearing that your schedule
Abounds with all good things,
Brings a smile to my face.
I bet that your heart sings.

Take a look around you.
View what you're grateful for.
Don't forget your "Thank You's"
To those that you adore.

Always bring your manners
Wherever you may go.
Know when to be humble.
A beauty, this does show.

Do your best and better.
Good things will come your way.
Please enjoy the moment
On each and every day.

CREATE YOUR WORLD

What we all are
What we will be
Depends upon
What we do see.

In life we know
That each day's news
Presents us with
Much varied views.

How we react
Each Time – Each Day
Does guide us through
Our journey's way.

The friends we make
In life do tell
Our choices made
That suit us well.

HUMILITY –
Along with Pride
Partner with each.
It shows we tried.

Success we find
Comes to us all.
Fond memories
We will recall.

Create your world
With all good things.
Enjoy the life
That friendship brings.

When joy is yours,
What makes you smile ?
With a warm heart,
Please share awhile.

PRECIOUS RAY OF SUNSHINE

A precious ray of sunshine
Now has come your way
To brighten up your life
On each and every day.

Embrace these tender moments
That now will fill your life,
But be aware of some things
That are sure to cause you strife.

Sleepless nights, and feeding times,
And thrush, and cradle cap,
Strange rashes, and some teething
Will hinder your day's nap.

Baby baths and fresh new clothes,
A clean fragrance that will stay
Until the air is scented with
Full diapers, Don't delay !

But when your finger is caressed
By such a little hand,
And a smile is sent your way,
You'll begin to understand

That life is such a precious gift.
Enjoy its every sound.
Embrace this life that comes to you.
For true happiness you have found.

ANOTHER FINE DAY

Another fine day
With sunshine and clouds –
A fiery sky –
Of the Earth it shrouds.

A sheet of fresh rain
With thunder we hear.
We thank you NATURE.
It's lightning we fear.

Our April May see
Some showers galore.
What was barren land
We now do adore.

For hidden beneath
A wealth full of dreams,
We see the blossoms
As our landscape gleams.

Beams of a rainbow
Enhance our view.
One wonders what NATURE
Will bring us that's new.

So many journeys
With so much to share –
We have a duty
To show that we care.

What lays a pathway
That reaches my heart
I will forever,
In life, not depart.

A PEACE OF MIND

Another Day
Another Star
Another Dream
Takes us afar.

Beyond our world
We seek to find
An atmosphere
With peace of mind.

Problems are More
Solutions – Few
Beyond is such
A different view.

A dream of dreams –
Just close your eyes
For then you'll see
The "where's" and "why's".

The "who's" and "what's"
Will become clear.
The peace you seek
Will be quite near.

Journey Taken –
A safe return –
Do share with all
What you did learn.

A distant view
As we look back –
A wonder of
What we did lack.

For happiness
In all we do
We seek to find –
Best We Review.

For maybe we'll
Just look around –
Then share with what
Our view has found.

Our journey far
Just needn't be –
For I found peace
Inside of me.

Your world is mine –
We all should share
Life's challenges
To show we care.

We'll travel "To"
And not "Away"
Toward the peace
We seek each day.

For our life now
Is where we are.
We light the night
As this world's star.

~Wishes~

A BETTER DAY

Am I the best that I can be ?
What exactly should I see ?
To let me know I'm on my way
To give our world a "Better Day ?"

A tender smile – A helping hand,
Shared with all throughout the land,
May give to some a little rest,
Surely, this is not my best.

For in my heart there is a glow,
But, much more I need to know.
The special talents we do share
Truly, make us more aware.

It's what we do to make things right,
Bringing sunshine to one's night,
Sometimes during the course of time
We forget what is sublime.

At times my life's put in review
For surely there is something new:
To be my best I do recall.
To be my best I honor all.

On my journey I do take PRIDE
For it can be a lonely ride.
HUMILITY should come our way
To give our world a "Better Day."

OUR HAPPINESS

Each day we look
For happiness.
We hope it comes
Our way.

Each day we wish
Our happiness
Will forever
Stay.

Each day we'll share
This happiness
With our Friends and
Foes.

Each day we'll ask
Our happiness
To travel
Unopposed.

My Day – Your Day,
Our memories
We know,
Will surely be,

Filled with joy.
It's wonderful !
Our love
We surely see.

MIDNIGHT MOONLIGHT

A whisper floated
Through the air
On a soft breeze
From everywhere.

An echo gently
Found its way
Through rainbow beams.
What does it say ?

A raindrop travels –
At Great Speed !
With many friends
It's Earth they feed.

Some chilly raindrops
Turn to snow.
Gently – Softly
We watch them flow.

Our Midnight Blue Moon
Fills the sky.
The shooting stars
Bring us a sigh.

Sunrise and Sunset
Every Day –
How fortunate
They don't delay.

While closing our eyes
Every night
Our dreams we see
With much delight.

The sun fills us
With Daylight Dreams
Which are quite clear,
Or so it seems.

We're lucky when a
Dream Comes True.
An Old Dream, we
Sometimes Renew.

Just fill our lives
With a Moon's Glow.
The sun will tell
Us where to go.

To lead and follow
We shall see
What life's about –
For you and me.

A CLOUD OF DREAMS

Thank you for sharing
What comes into view –
Your moment in time
for all to review.

A Cloud filled with dreams,
You've choices to make,
New lessons to learn,
Journeys to partake.

There are smiles to be made.
Bows will come your way.
Some contracts you'll sign
To ensure your pay.

When we visit next
Much Older we'll be –
More wisdom to share
For more life we did see.

I YEARN TO LEARN

I dream a dream
Most every day
That all good things
Will come my way.

Both small and large –
No special size –
I feel my dreams
May make me wise.

I joke of course
For I'm not sure
When wisdom comes
And does endure.

Of course I know
What I don't know.
The trick I see
Is not to show.

How wise I'm not
Until I learn
The knowledge that
My mind does yearn.

I won't pretend.
I'll listen well
To what I hear –
To what they tell.

This brings to me
A peace of mind.
I realize I'm
One of a kind.

Just like us all
We tend to be
That you are you
For I am me.

I'll just relax –
Truly I know
Much love I have
Where I do go.

Caress the place
Where you are now.
Your efforts – PLEASE
Do take a Bow !

GRADUATION DREAMS

Be proud dear friend
In what you do.
Enjoy what's old.
Caress what's new.

So many hats
In life you'll wear,
A selfless life
Because you care.

For every night
There'll be a dream.
By morning light
Your view will seem

To challenge you.
Accept what's clear.
Help those in need,
Both far and near.

You've much to share –
Talents galore !
Be kind to all.
Your life will soar.

A rainbow bright,
You are our star
Lighting the sky
Both near and far.

Some days you know
Should disappear.
Those you do love
Will share your tear.

In life you'll take
All that you dare.
Remember please,
Your talents share.

Your smiles will come.
Sometimes they'll go.
Life's better when
You share your glow.

Your loved ones are
So proud to say
Their love they send
To you each day.

Don't hesitate
If help you need.
Just look our way.
We're yours, indeed.

Forget us not.
Your pot of gold
Will always be
For you to hold.

MAKE A WISH

Make one wish
Or two Or three,
Your wish list
Does excite me.

Travel near.
Now travel far.
Each book read
Makes you a STAR.

Every word,
A story's told.
New worlds will,
To you, unfold.

Take along
Your Mother Dear.
Keep your love
For her so near.

Show a smile
Give Mom a hug.
Always bc
Her precious bug.

INTO THE NIGHT

No fear my dear.
The day shines bright.
Our sun brings you
Into the night.

It's time to dream.
With stars in view,
Each night will show
What is so new.

Your voyage may
Travel so far
That you may want
To squeeze a star.

Each step you take,
Each thought you keep,
Will serve you well,
This crop you reap.

The challenge is,
When your eyes wake,
If you can write
Your "dream" remake.

On your nightstand
Please keep a pad.
With pen in hand,
You'll be quite glad.

We'd love to read
Your dreams come true.
Be proud ! Enjoy
The work you do.

OUR SPECIAL DISH

Wonders are ahead of you.
Many dreams you'll see come true.
Grade Four was a special year.
Now Grade Five will soon be here.

Summer fun and books to read,
New skills learned; your mind you'll feed.
Ice cream cones, a lick or two,
Drips down on what you do do.

Minutes spent most every day,
Memorize your tables, EH !
Then reverse what you do know.
Dividing now is what you show.

Splash some water on your face
You and Nana have a race.
Noodles Ready ! One ! Two ! Three !
Goggles Tight ! Now you can see !

Sing a song; Direct a play.
Write a script of words to say.
Do some baking. Cook a meal.
Study maps of places real.

List some household chores you do.
Be helpful. Add something new.
See a movie. Go dine out.
Sit up front and ride about.

Enjoy every day that's here
And remember you're our dear.
Sweet Dreams for you we do wish
Because you are our Special Dish.

I WISH FOR YOU

There was a time
Not long ago
That in my heart
Much love did flow.

Each morning brought
A calming day
That placed me on
A rainbow's ray.

For all around
Just smiles I'd see
That magically
Would comfort me.

When clouds appeared
To spoil my view
I always thought
Of what to do.

My eyes I'd close
Dreams would appear.
A peaceful peace
Would be quite near.

Fond memories
Would clear My Sky.
Onward I'd go –
Higher I'd fly !

I wish for you
On your life's flight
That joy is yours
Both day and night.

Old memories
That you now view
May be replaced
With something new.

Your journey now
And evermore
Will be a life
That you adore.

Please let us share
All that will be
Enjoying Life
Eternally !

RESPECT

In spirit honor seniors
For all that they have done
To ensure your happiness
Where in life they had none.

Lend a helping hand each day.
To your cell phone, give a rest.
Knowing you give to yourself
A bit of life that's best.

Listen to your elders please
For history books they are.
Even though they may "repeat"
Make them your precious star.

"Record" sessions you do share.
You'll cherish what you hear.
In the future you may crave
The voice of one so dear.

To all do bring some laughter.
Greet elders with a smile.
Share some of your life's history
Along with your lifestyle.

Careers you may consider
Are topics to relate.
The highway you might travel
Will have more than one gate.

Tomorrow isn't promised.
Today is what you see.
Caress those tender moments
That form your memory.

ENJOY YOUR DREAMS

With pen in hand
Some thoughts I seek.
They may be bold.
Some may be meek.

A moral shared –
Preaching, I'm not.
So many years –
Lessons we're taught.

What's good for me
May not apply
To everyone –
I don't deny.

Regrets for sure
Have filled my dreams –
A haunting of
What's real, it seems.

So many times
A smile or two
Accompanied
With "I Love You"

Would make the day
A pleasant one
For Mom and Dad
And for their Son.

By knowing what
Is right and wrong
Builds Character –
Makes people strong.

I try in life
To be aware
Of people's needs
To show I care.

I try to see
What I would do
If you were I
And I were you.

So many times
In life I greet
A chance to solve
Problems I meet.

Some Large – Some Small
With help near me
A calm is felt
From what I see.

I hesitate
Before I speak.
A gentle word
Is what I seek.

Too quick sometimes
We don't think through
How we could help
Life in review.

Slow Down – Relax
Enjoy the Day
For all good things
Will come our way.

Don't just receive –
Know when to give.
Enjoy Your Dreams
Make our Life Live.

We're on a stage.
The role we play
Will, from the heart,
Our love relay.

YOU WARM OUR HEARTS

You warm our hearts
Most every day
By what you do
And what you say.

The choices made,
As you advance,
Provides you with
Most every chance,

To share your dreams,
As you explore
Your visions of
What you adore.

We welcome when
You look our way
And ask for help
Throughout the day.

You know we know
Not everything
But there are times
That our words bring

The right ideas
For you to try.
Success will come,
We won't deny.

Setting new goals,
We're sure you'll do
Most every day,
For dreams come true.

So make a wish
And dream a dream.
Enjoy your world.
Just watch it gleam.

Include us in
Your brilliant glow.
Remember that
We love you so.

A PRECIOUS VIEW

Every time I close my eyes
A dream I do begin.
Travel with me, knowing that
My dreams come from within.

Your smile shared with me today
With pleasant thoughts galore,
Was a darling moment which
Left me wanting more.

Eyes were met and hands were held.
A long and gentle hug
Filled your presence in my dream.
My heart caressed your tug.

Thank you for this cherished view,
The love you sent my way.
Always in my dreams my dear,
Will be this precious day.

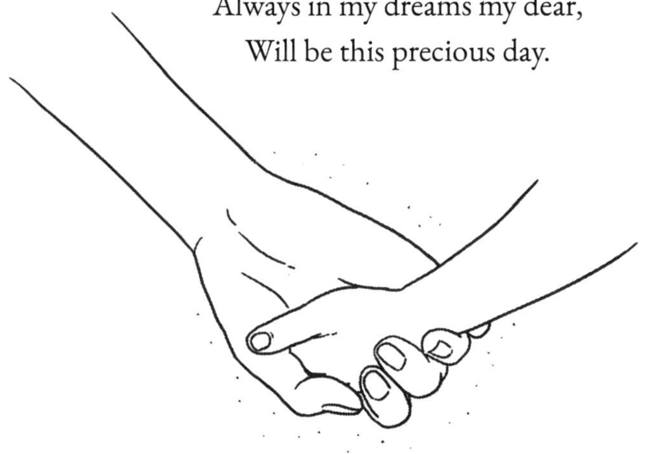

HAPPY EVERYTHING

So many thoughts
So many dreams
Do come to life,
Or so it seems.

Which way to look
Which way to turn –
Decisions made –
So much to learn.

Careers sometimes
Are hard to choose.
I'll try them all.
What's there to lose ?

I'll match my skills.
I'll learn some more.
Life's challenges,
I do adore.

There's joy to seek
With much to love.
I welcome all
From up above.

ABOUT THE AUTHOR

Robert G. LaPointe is a distinguished educator and prolific poet who lives in a rhyming world. He dedicated over 35 years to teaching 4th grade in northern New York and was honored with the Outstanding Elementary Teachers of America Award in 1973.

Robert began writing poems as a shy boy trying to win smiles and hearts through verse. This passion evolved into a lifelong endeavor, channeling his creativity to bring laughter, encouragement, and care with his words. Inspired by dreams, experiences, and goals, Robert's poems capture heartfelt memories and humbly share life lessons. He frequently gifts poems to family and friends, cherishing every smile or tear from his audience.

Over the past 20 years, Robert has penned countless poems as "Poppy the Poet" for his granddaughter, Claire Elyce, each poem lovingly typed by his wife, Norma, aka "Nana the Typist." Aiming to cultivate listening skills, spark imagination, and foster respect for seniors, Robert's poetry resonates with readers of all ages.

Made in the USA
Columbia, SC
07 November 2024